Jungle Animals

Written by Cathy Jones
Reading consultants: Christopher Collier and Alan Howe,
Bath Spa University, UK

First published by Parragon in 2009
Parragon
Queen Street House
4 Queen Street
Bath BA1 1HE, UK

ISBN 978-1-4075-8858-2

Printed in China

Jungle Animals

LIVE. LEARN. DISCOVER.

Bath New York Singapore Hong Kong Cologne Delhi Melbourne

Parents' notes

This book is part of a series of nonfiction books designed to appeal to children learning to read.

Each book has been developed with the help of educational experts.

At the end of each book is a quiz to help your child remember the information and the meanings of some of the words and sentences. There is also a glossary of difficult words relating to the subject matter in the book, and an index.

Contents

Life in the jungle

vampire bat

The jungle is a hot, steamy forest. It is also called the **rain forest**. Tall trees grow up to 230 feet above the forest floor. The rain can take 20 minutes to reach the ground.

The forest floor is dark because the tree branches block out the sun.

DiscoveryFact™

There are almost 10 million species of animal living in the rain forest, but only about 1.5 million have been named.

Birds nest and bats roost in the tallest trees.

Apes, monkeys, and sloths climb in the canopy.

• Snakes, frogs, and **insects** live in the branches and trunks.

• Wild cats, anteaters, elephants, and other large animals prowl the forest floor.

• Crocodiles, turtles, and fish swim in the swamps and rivers.

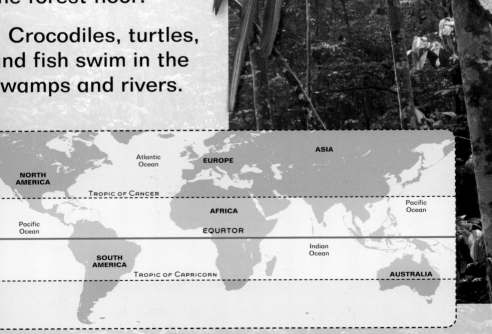

Rain forests grow between the tropics and the equator, the hottest part of the earth.

Jungle animals

All kinds of animals live in the jungle, such as **mammals**, **reptiles**, birds, and fish. Insects are the largest group of animals in the jungle.

Some animals have **adapted** so well to life in the jungle that they cannot live anywhere else.

Mammals, such as the golden lion tamarin, are covered with fur and feed

golden lion tamarin

The Indian gharial is a reptile. It hunts for fish in the river. It lays eggs on dry land.

The harpy eagle is probably the largest flying rain forest bird. Its feathery wings measure up to 6½ feet when they are spread out. It can carry away a monkey or sloth in its long talons.

9

Hunter and hunted

Life in the jungle can be hard. Animals that eat plants and insects are hunted by small meat-eating animals. These small animals are hunted by bigger **predators**.

The jaguar's spotted coat acts as **camouflage**. It eats other animals, such as the giant anteater.

The giant anteater has a long snout and sticky tongue—good for scooping up ants

rhinoceros beetle

Leaf-cutter ants can carry leaves 50 times heavier than themselves. They bury pieces of leaf and eat the **fungus** that grows on them.

DiscoveryFact™

The poison dart frog is a brightly colored **amphibian**. Its bright colors warn enemies that it is poisonous to eat.

The Amazon

The largest rain forest in the world is in South America around the Amazon River. It is filled with a lot of colorful life.

Capybaras belong to the same rodent family as mice and rats. They grow up to 2 feet tall.

DiscoveryFact™

Vampire bats feed on the blood of other animals.

The colorful, noisy toucan has a strong beak. It can easily open nutshells to eat the kernel inside.

The anaconda is the heaviest snake in the world. It can grow to 37 feet long. It squeezes its **prey** to death, then eats it whole.

The rhinoceros beetle is the strongest animal in the world because it can carry 850 times its own weight. It grows to over 2 inches long.

Monkeys

Monkeys are **primates**, like us. They have hands like ours with thumbs that bend away from their fingers. Their eyes are at the front of their head. They live in family groups called troops.

These chimpanzees are grooming each other to keep clean and to relax.

The largest monkey in the world is the mandrill. It grows up to about 3 feet tall. The male mandrill has a colorful face and bottom, which get brighter when it is excited.

The owl monkey is the only monkey that is active at night and sleeps in the day. Its big eyes help it see in the dark.

The smallest monkey in the world is the pygmy marmoset. It is only 6 inches long, not counting its 7-inch long tail.

The Congo

The Congo is the second largest rain forest in the world. Running through the rain forest is the second largest river in the world, the Congo River.

Gorillas jaguar closest relatives in the animal world. They spend most of their time on the ground, walking on their knuckles for support.

Like its relative the giraffe, the okapi has a very long giant millepede ing food from high trees giant tree frog ushes.

A chameleon changes the color of its skin to blend into the surroundings if it feels threatened.

rpy eagle

naconda

nt anteater

argay   okapi   chameleon

e kangaroo   Bengal tiger   peacock   cassowary

angutan   water dragon

celot   gorilla   toucan   mandrill

louded leopard giant black millipede can grow to 15 inches and has two pairs of legs on each segment of its body.

Wild cats

Rain forest cats are hunters. They hunt alone at night. They have good night vision and mark the forest trails with their **scent** to warn off other animals.

Tigers are piranha fish cats in the world. The Bengal tiger can grow up to 10 feet long. It hunts for wild boar, oxen, and monkeys.

DiscoveryFact™

The margay spends its whole life in the trees hunting birds and monkeys.

The clouded leopard is a good climber. It can run down a tree trunk headfirst.

The ocelot may look like a pet cat, but it is twice as big. It is also very fierce. It hunts small deer, rabbits, and fish.

Indonesia

owl monkey is a ribbon of 17,000 islands in the Indian ocean. About one-half of the land is covered in jungle. There are over 3,500 species of ani poison dart frog .

Orangutans live in the rain forest trees. At night, they make a nest to sleep in. They eat mainly fruit.

The deadly king cobra grows up to 18 feet long. Its two fangs can inject poison into its prey.

The peacock raises its magnificent tail feathers to attract a peahen to mate with.

The water dragon is 2 feet long. It can run away quickly on its back legs and hide underwater for up to 90 minutes.

Snakes

Rain forest snakes are good at hiding. They slither under fallen leaves, hide in hollow tree trunks, and wind themselves around overhanging branches. They smell prey by flicking their tongue.

The cobra is a poisonous snake. When it is in danger, it makes itself look bigger by raising its head and puffing out its hood.

The deadly coral snake lives in the trees and on the forest floor. One bite from this viper snake is enough to kill an adult. It grows up to 3 feet long.

The green tree snake finds its food in the trees, swallowing frogs and lizards headfirst.

Australia

The Australian rain forest is home to many animals that are not seen in the bandicoot the world.

bandicoot

DiscoveryFact™

The cassowary is the largest land animal in Australia at 5 feet tall. It is a bird but it cannot fly.

Tree kangaroos are good climbers and can jump from branch to branch. The baby kangaroo, called a joey, is carried in its mother's belly pouch.

The giant tree frog is the biggest tree frog in the world. It grows up to 4 inches long.

Indian gharial oo, the bandicoot carries its babies in a pouch. The bandicoot's pouch is on its back instead of its stomach.

Quiz

Now try this quiz!

All the answers can be found in this book.

Which snake squeezes its prey to death?

(a) Anaconda
(b) Coral snake
(c) Green tree snake

Which monkey is the smallest?

(a) Chimpanzee
(b) Pygmy marmoset
(c) Owl monkey

Why does a chameleon change the color of its skin?

(a) For fun
(b) When it feels threatened
(c) To attract a mate

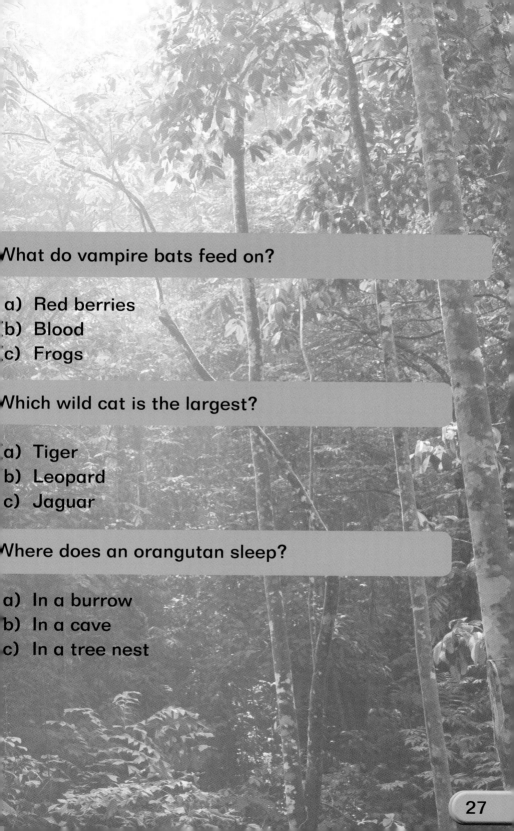

What do vampire bats feed on?

a) Red berries
b) Blood
c) Frogs

Which wild cat is the largest?

a) Tiger
b) Leopard
c) Jaguar

Where does an orangutan sleep?

a) In a burrow
b) In a cave
c) In a tree nest

Glossary

Adapted   Changed in a way that helps the animal to survive where it lives.

Amphibian   A group of animals (such as frogs) that lay eggs in water and can live on land.

Camouflage   An animal's pattern or color that helps it hide against the background.

Fungus   A living thing a little like a plant. Fungi are not green. Mushrooms and toadstools are fungi.

Insect   A group of small animals with six legs. Many insects have wings.

Mammal   A group of animals that have a backbone, give birth to babies, and feed them milk.

Predator   An animal that hunts another animal for food.

Prey   An animal that is hunted by another animal for food.

Primate   A group of animals that includes humans, monkeys, and apes.

Rain forest   An area of evergreen forest near the tropics where there is a lot of rainfall.

Reptile   A group of animals covered with scales that includes lizards, snakes, and crocodiles.

Scent   The smell that an animal leaves to tell other animals it has been in a place.

Index

Acknowledgments

t=top, c=center, b=bottom, r=right, l=left

Front cover: Getty Images/Andy Rouse
Back cover: l Getty Images/Laura Wickenden, r Getty Images/
Cyril Laubscher

1 istockphoto/ Kenneth O'Quinn, 2 Getty Images/ William Weber,
3 istockphoto/ Erik van Hannen, 4 istockphoto/Tokle, 5 tl istockphoto/
Erik van Hannen, 5 cl Getty Images/ Frans Lemmens, 5 br Getty
Images/Joel Sartore, 6-7 istockphoto/ SZE FEI WONG,
6bl istockphoto/ Kenneth O'Quinn, 7 tr istockphoto/ Finn Brandt,
8-9 istockphoto/ ray roper, 8 b istockphoto/ Erik van Hannen,
9 cl Getty Images/Joel Sartore, 9 cr istockphoto/Simon Podgorsek,
10-11 Getty Images/Tim Laman, 10 cl istockphoto/Sondra Paulson,
10 b Getty Images/Peter Lilja, 11 br istockphoto/Steve Geer,
12-13 Getty Images/M G Therin Weise, 12 br istockphoto/Michael
Lynch, 13 tr istockphoto/Roberto A Sanchez, 13 cl Getty Images/Gary
Braasch, 13 br istockphoto/Tokle, 14-15 Getty Images/VEER John
Giustina, 14 cl istockphoto/Catharina van den Dikkenberg,
15 tr Getty Images/Art Wolfe, 15 cr istockphoto/Michael Lynch,
16-17 istockphoto/Guenter Guni, 16 cl istockphoto/Gary Martin,
16bl istockphoto/Kenneth O'Quinn, 17 br AFP/Getty Images,
18-19 Getty Images/Jami Tarris, 18 br Getty Images/Carol Farneti-
Foster, 19 tr istockphoto/dieter Spears, 19cr Getty Images/Tom
Brakefield, 20-21istockphoto/George Clerk, 20 br Getty Images/Tom
Brakefield, 21 br Getty Images/Frans Lemmens, 22 Getty Images/
Bnsdeo, 23 cl Getty Images/William Weber, 23 tr Getty Images/
Jim Merli, 23 b Getty Images/Joel Sartore, 24-25 istockphoto/
susan flashman, 24 bl Getty Images/Jason Edwards, 25tr National
Geographic/Getty Images